FORT LAUDERDALE
The Delaplaine
2021 Long Weekend Guide

Andrew Delaplaine

Senior Editor - *Renee Delaplaine*
Senior Writer - **James Cubby**

Gramercy Park Press
New York London Paris

Please submit corrections, additions or comments to
andrewdelaplaine@mac.com

TABLE OF CONTENTS

Chapter 1
WHY FORT LAUDERDALE?

Fort Lauderdale, for good or ill, has always been defined not for what it is, really, as for what it lies between. About 40 miles to the north is Palm Beach. About 25 miles south is Miami. A million images flood the mind when you think of Miami. (Cocaine Cowboys, the Mariel Boatlift, South Beach, the nightlife, Little Havana, an international port and banking center.) Similarly, a million images leap into your mind when you conjure up Palm Beach (Worth Avenue, Cartier, the Kennedys, wealthy socialites, vast fortunes, elderly women with young gigolos.)

And Fort Lauderdale? What images jump into your mind when you first think of the town? Connie Francis and "Where the Boys Are"? Spring Break? Sailboats?

Well, Fort Lauderdale has come a long way since that 1960 movie.

And the good thing that has made Fort Lauderdale so attractive for so long is that it is *not* Miami and it is *not* Palm Beach. It's just that "little bit of in between" that makes Fort Lauderdale so great. And, being in the middle of the Gold Coast, Fort Lauderdale is a perfect location if you like Miami or Palm Beach, but don't want to live there. You're just a few minutes away by I-95 or the Turnpike from posh Palm Beach or the nonstop excitement of Miami.

Wonderful smaller towns (Davie, Dania, Lauderdale-by-the-Sea, Lighthouse Point) offer extremely cheap housing (if you want to live here) and lodgings, if you're visiting. And you're close-close-close to all the action. (I know a lot of actors who live in these towns for the very reason that they are easily able to go to auditions in Miami or Palm Beach. When they get jobs, they're never too far away.)

Specific Information During Your Visit

BROWARD-PALM BEACH *NEW TIMES*
www.broggwardpalmbeach.com
This weekly freebie paper is available on almost every street corner in boxes—you definitely need to

get a copy to see what's going on the week or two you're in town. Online you'll find thousands of listings that will help you work your way through the town.

SUN-SENTINEL
www.sun-sentinel.com
This is the local daily newspaper, but only its Friday and Sunday editions have information of use to the visitor. The web site is a big help.

Visitors' Centers

**THE GREATER FORT LAUDERDALE
CONVENTION & VISITORS BUREAU**
954-765-4466.
www.sunny.org
Has complete listings.

Chapter 2
LODGING

BEACH AREA

It's very true what they say. Fort Lauderdale has a beach for everyone! After all, this is what you are really coming to Fort Lauderdale to enjoy. Isn't it?

ATLANTIC HOTEL

601 N. Ft. Lauderdale Beach Blvd, 954-567-8020
www.atlantichotelfl.com
This smallish property (124 rooms & suites) right on the water has a lot to recommend it: a causal décor

that remains stylish while not being stuffy like the **W** or the **Ritz**. (About half the rooms have full kitchens). Also has the **Spa Atlantic**, sea-and-citrus inspired day spa. As a splendidly relaxing destination, his sanctuary uses products made from natural ingredients. Deep-tissue massage, revitalizing body scrub in one of 8 private treatment rooms, Swedish massage, in-suite massages, aromatherapy massage. Also, a couples treatment room. Also offers a spectrum of refreshing facial, professional salon services and beauty treatments.

BAHIA MAR BEACH RESORT
801 Seabreeze Blvd., Fort Lauderdale: 954-764-2233
www.bahiamarhotel.com
This 40-acre beachfront retreat is within walking distance of Las Olas Boulevard with the area's shopping, dining and **Riverwalk** entertainment.

COURTYARD BY MARRIOTT
440 Seabreeze Blvd., Fort Lauderdale Beach: 954-524-8733
www.marriott.com
If you want the same-old, same-old, here it is.

GALT VILLAS
3621 N. Ocean Blvd., Fort Lauderdale: 954-563-3400
www.galtvillas.com
Right across the street from the beach. Great rates; rooms and efficiencies; daily, weekly, monthly; pool, 27" TVs with 70 channels; in-room coffee maker with free coffee; mini-fridge & microwave; rollaway beds,

cribs, ironing boards, coin laundry, free Internet station.

GRANADA INN
3011 Granada St., Fort Lauderdale: 954-463-2032
www.granadainn.net
The Granada Inn is an open-balcony Caribbean art deco style **bed and breakfast** located just a few short steps from the beach. The continental breakfast is served poolside, which is surrounded by palm trees and a tropical garden.

HYATT REGENCY PIER 66
2301 S.E. 17th St. Cswy., Fort Lauderdale: 954-525-6666
www.pier66hotelmarina.com
The famous **Pier 66** property with its distinctive rooftop restaurant. Newly renovated (2009) and located in a 22-acre, lushly landscaped property 3 miles from the airport, 3 blocks from the beach (they have a free shuttle) and 10 minutes from downtown. Has a very impressive Spa. (There's a Sunday Brunch in the restaurant on top that's as real treat. The views

are outstanding.) One of the big treats about this place is you've got lot of marina action. Fort Lauderdale is famous as a yachting center (unlike Miami), so you're constantly surrounded by boat people. A lot of them hang out here.

LAGO MAR RESORT
http://www.lagomar.com/
1700 S. Ocean Ln., Fort Lauderdale: 954-523-6511
This luxury resort features 475 feet of private sandy beach, a 9,000 sq. ft. swimming lagoon and 2 tennis courts. Play a game of chess on the life-sized outdoor chess set. It's situated between Lake Mayan and the ocean on a 10-acre plot that's lushly landscaped. Great yacht watching. Lots of the rooms and suites here have full kitchens. Has lots of on-site activities (putt-putt golf, tennis, beach volleyball, shuffleboard, playground and that very huge pool), making it a popular destination for families. Also excellent on-site dining.

MARRIOTT'S BEACHPLACE TOWERS
21 S. Fort Lauderdale Beach Blvd., Fort Lauderdale: 954-525-4440
www.marriott.com
Between the waters of the Atlantic & Intracoastal Waterway, Marriott's BeachPlace Towers gives you the full-on Marriott treatment. They have spacious one- and two-bedroom villas or deluxe guestrooms situated atop three floors of retail shops & restaurants. (The villas feature separate living and dining areas, large master suites with king beds and oversized

soaking tubs, full kitchens with cookware and tableware, utility rooms with washer/dryer.)

THE PILLARS
111 N. Birch Rd., Fort Lauderdale: 954-467-9639
www.pillarshotel.com
Hidden away off the beach is this genuine find. Walk out to the tropically landscaped pool area that overlooks the Intracoastal. No better place to relax than this place, and once you've stayed here, you'll be telling everybody you know about it in a way that will cause everyone to envy you. It's places like this that make you want to avoid the **Ritz-Carlton** and the **W** and all the other properties in the thick of things. Why? Because this place is different. You get the

feeling (OK, it's fleeting) that you've gone back in time to some Colonial outpost in the Caribbean. This impression is enhanced when you get a room with French doors. (Ask for one.) The furnishings are refined (rich dark woods, elegant upholstery) and comfortable. There's a restaurant here where it's divine to sit at night overlooking the Intracoastal as the yachts go by. (None of your noisy beach traffic here, thank you very much.) Eatery is called the **Secret Garden**. Breakfast and lunch are served only to hotel guests. At dinner they allow outsiders to come in, those who are members of the Secret Garden Society, the hotel's private dining club. (Call or email them at secretgarden@pillarshotel.com to see if they'll let you squeeze in for dinner.)

RITZ-CARLTON FORT LAUDERDALE RESORT

1 N. Fort Lauderdale Beach Blvd., Fort Lauderdale Beach: 954-465-2300
www.ritzcarlton.com
Ritz-Carlton Spa (with 8500 square feet) features private treatment rooms, separate lounges for men and women, cardiovascular and strength equipment in the fitness room; 11 treatment rooms including private couple's treatment suite; private massage areas and Jacuzzis on the tropical pool deck; fitness center with Technogym cardiovascular and strength equipment; Spa boutique. 24 hour business center. Many of the niceties you'd expect from a Ritz-Carlton property. A private little skywalk that takes you to the beach. A huge wine cellar. A "pampered pooch" special for dogs (under 25 lbs.) offers a special dog bed in your room so Fido won't feel left out of all the fun. The excellent **Via Luna** restaurant is located here.

SEA LORD HOTEL & SUITES

4140 El Mar Dr., Lauderdale-by-the-Sea: 954-776-1505
www.sealordhotel.com
On 150 feet of beach. The pool deck overlooks the ocean. This property was renovated in 2002. Perfectly nice mid-range property.

SEVILLE HOTEL

3020 Seville St., Fort Lauderdale: 954-463-7212
http://seville-hotel-and-apartments.miami-metropolitan-area.com

Located in the heart of the beach district and just steps away from restaurants, entertainment, water taxis and shopping. The Seville offers efficiencies & apartments with fully equipped kitchens as well as hotel rooms with fridge & microwaves.

TROPIROCK RESORT
2900 Belmar St., Fort Lauderdale: 954-565-5790
www.tropirockresort-fl.us
A 3 or 4 minute walk from the beach. The Tropirock features handcrafted designer furnishings, colorful Caribbean art fusion and a highly trained multilingual staff. The landscaping is unique in the sense that it's totally UN-corporate. Funky. Exotic. Winding pathways take to you citrus trees, banana trees and coconut palms, papaya, fragrant jasmine and blooming passion vines. Throughout the property you'll run into a series of mosaics that add to the artistic sensibility they're going for here. Terra cotta suns, chips of reflective glass, broken dishware, seashells and chunks of coral in a stucco mix all surrounded by lush tropical landscaping.

W HOTEL FORT LAUDERDALE
401 N. Fort Lauderdale Beach Blvd., Fort
Lauderdale: 954-414-8200
www.marriott.com
Hard to call it a "boutique" hotel with over 400
rooms, but it tries to be one while trading on its
endlessly hip image. The concierge with the
"whenever/whatever" service. Reminds me of that
Noel Coward song, "The Passenger's Always Right,"
with the lyric: "The passenger's always right, my dear
/ the passenger's always right. / The son of a bitch is
probably rich, / so smile with all your might." But all
cattiness aside, the place is a dream. Right on the
water. Beautifully designed rooms. Has **Steak 954** on
site, as well as luxurious **Bliss Spa**.

WESTIN BEACH RESORT FORT LAUDERDALE

321 N. Fort Lauderdale Beach Blvd., Fort Lauderdale: 954-467-1111
www.westin.com

Tropically decorated rooms, 2 pools, recreation program, pool bar & grill, 2 lounges and live entertainment nightly. From the third-floor pool deck overlooking the water, there's a skywalk that you use to get to the beach. There's a **Heavenly Spa by Westin**, a 6,500-square-foot space with separate men's and women's Jacuzzis, steam rooms, and locker rooms. Spa treatments before or after exercise—the Heavenly Spa is located on the resort's first floor right across from the WestinWORKOUT Gym. Great place for the athletic among you. A short drive away is the **Jimmy Evert Tennis Center**, an outstanding public tennis center with 18 lighted clay courts and 3 hard courts, plus locker rooms, a lounge, pro shop, racquet re-stringing, and more. Refine your game with expert private lessons, or just practice your swings on your own by renting a ball machine. There's also the **Westin Kids Club**. On arrival, kids from four to 12 years old get an adventure-bound amenity bag to get them excited about their visit. The hotel has a "Discovery Room" where endless diversions from board games, arts and crafts, and even a Nintendo Wii will keep them occupied for hours. Healthy meals and snacks are provided, and a professional staff supervises a range of activities, including off-site excursions—so parents can relax and enjoy the resort themselves, worry-free.

WestinWORKOUT Gym offers 1,425 square feet of

space: a full array of strength-training equipment and free weights; cardio machines—treadmills, elliptical trainers, step machines, and stationary bikes all offer personal flat screen TVs. Ocean views out the windows offer further inspiration. The gym is open 24 hours a day to resort guests 16 years and older, complimentary and accessible with any guest room key. Towels and headphones are also provided.

DOWNTOWN AREA

The downtown area, especially around Las Olas Boulevard, has seen quite a bit of development in the past decade, and now hosts many new hotels and high-rise condominium developments. The downtown area is the largest in Broward County. My favorite hotel is still the quaint and charming **Riverside**. It's been upgraded, renovated and I'm not too pleased with the public rooms, but what the hell. I always get a room in the old section of the property.

HAMPTON INN FT. LAUDERDALE DOWNTOWN
250 N. Andrews Ave., Fort Lauderdale: 954-924-2700
www.hamptoninn3.hilton.com
The Hampton Inn Ft. Lauderdale Downtown features room service, a pool area, a multi-lingual staff and an exercise room. But boring, boring, boring.

RIVERSIDE HOTEL

620 E. Las Olas Blvd., Fort Lauderdale: 954-467-0671

www.riversidehotel.com

If you're going to be downtown, by all means stay here. It used to be my favorite hotel in Fort Lauderdale (that's not on the beach). Built in 1936, it's the oldest hotel in town, and they've added a 12-floor tower, but I prefer the older rooms. They call them "traditional rooms." Still, the rooms in the tower (big at 500 square feet) offer commanding views of the New River and all of downtown. I'm not at all happy with the way they've "upgraded" the dining room and the bars. Everything's ugly and generic, but it's still better than most places. And you're in the middle of Las Olas, the only really interesting street with any character in the whole town.

GAY LODGINGS

Greater Fort Lauderdale has more than 150 gay-owned establishments including hotels, bars, clubs and restaurants, as well as three gay and lesbian publications and the largest Metropolitan Community Church congregation in the United States. While Fort Lauderdale is full of gay people, the focal point is Wilton Manors and Oakland Park. (These lodgings are either gay owned, gay operated or gay-friendly.)

THE ALCAZAR RESORT
555 N. Birch Rd., Fort Lauderdale: 954-563-6819
http://www.alcazarresort.com
The Alcazar is a gay males only resort featuring a clothing optional courtyard 24-hour heated pool. Formerly **Sea Chateau Motel**.

CAMBRIA SUITES
141 SW 19th Court, Dania Beach: 954-889-2600
www.cambriasuitesfortlauderdale.com
All suite hotel in Dania Beach. Oversized suites with luxurious bedding and upscale amenities like flat-screen televisions and spa-like baths featuring Bath and Body Works amenities.

CORAL REEF GUESTHOUSE
2609 N.E. 13th Ct., Fort Lauderdale: 954-568-0292
http://www.coralreefguesthouse.com
Gay-owned and operated, offering male accommodations close to the beach, restaurants and the Galleria Mall. Rooms are tastefully decorated, and overlook the clothing optional heated pool and 14-man Jacuzzi.

CRUISE SHIP DEPARTURE STAYS
Port Everglades is the huge cruise port at Fort Lauderdale, Florida. The popular departure port serves millions of smiling cruise passengers every year.

RED CARPET INN
2460 W. State Rd. 84, Fort Lauderdale: 954-792-4700
www.redcarpetinns.com
The Red Carpet Inn features a pool area and airport transportation.

HOLIDAY INN EXPRESS AIR AND SEA PORT
1150 W. State Rd. 84, Fort Lauderdale: 954-828-9905
www.hiexpress.com

Just a mile from the Fort Lauderdale - Hollywood Int'l Airport (FLL).

Every morning the property offers free USA Today and the complimentary, hot Express Start Breakfast Bar with delicious cinnamon rolls.

FOUR POINTS BY SHERATON FORT LAUDERDALE AIRPORT/CRUISE PORT

1800 S. Federal Hwy., Fort Lauderdale: 954-767-8700

www.marriott.com

This hotel offers free airport and cruise port transportation, a free expanded deluxe continental breakfast featuring a Belgium Waffle station and is within walking distance to restaurants and shopping.

CROWNE PLAZA FORT LAUDERDALE AIRPORT / CRUISE PORT

455 State Rd. 84, Fort Lauderdale: 954-523-8080

www.crowneplaza.com

This hotel features room service, a swimming pool, airport transportation and a multi-lingual staff.

Chapter 3
RESTAURANTS

There's no question that Fort Lauderdale has an abundance of dining opportunities situated on the water. You'd think in Florida that this would normally be the case, but it is not. In South Beach, let's say, there's only a handful of restaurants on the water. (All those restaurants lining Ocean Drive? They're all a five-minute walk across the park and beach to the water.)

But here in Fort Lauderdale, it's all about the water. You have restaurants actually on the beach. You have them in marinas overflowing with yachts from around the world. You have them on the Waterway.

15TH STREET FISHERIES
1900 SE 15th St., Fort Lauderdale: 954-763-2777
http://www.15streetfisheries.com
CUISINE: Seafood
DRINKS: Full Bar
SERVING: Lunch/ Dinner
Right on the water with amazing views, this place is
cozy yet unpretentious. The lounge has a lower priced
menu (than the room upstairs) that includes alligator
burgers. The staff is friendly and knowledgeable, and
if the menu seems a little pricey, remember that salad
and an appetizer are included. $$$$

3030 OCEAN
3030 Holiday Dr., Fort Lauderdale: 954-765-3030
http://www.3030ocean.com
CUISINE: Seafood
DRINKS: Full Bar
SERVING: Dinner
Located in the Harbour Beach Marriott, at the helm of
this restaurant is runner-up to *Hell's Kitchen,* Paula
da Silva. Here she proves to be a winner with her
progressive yet tasty menu. The tuna tartare? Best in
town. The menu changes often as she likes to keep
serving the freshest seafood with the freshest
ingredients possible. $$$$

ANTHONY'S RUNWAY 84
330 State Road 84, Fort Lauderdale: 954-467-8484
http://runway-84.com
CUISINE: Italian
DRINKS: Full Bar
SERVING: Lunch/Dinner
This place has a feel of old Fort Lauderdale; that's a good thing. You must have the warm bread served with a cheese and olive oil dip that's to die for. Also on the menu are pizzas, but your best bet is to stick with the traditional Italian favorites. $$$$

ACQUARIO
LAGO MAR RESORT
http://www.lagomar.com/
1700 S. Ocean Ln., Fort Lauderdale: 954-523-6511
CUISINE: Varied; they call it "American bistro."
DRINKS: Full bar.
SERVING: dinner nightly.

Really excellent eatery here at Lago Mar, whatever the hell they call the cuisine. Try the butternut squash ravioli, pan roasted chicken, garlic lemon basil sauce ($22), the cherrywood plank salmon, pomegranate honey glazed, coarse boursin cheese grits ($22), shrimp & mussel garganelli with wilted greens, lemongrass lobster sauce ($29), or the hog snapper, cashew crusted, plantain jasmine rice, citrus butter sauce ($29). Or, really decadent: braised boneless short ribs, with root mashed, lemongrass Myers rum sauce ($32). The desserts are great, but skip them.

BISTRO MEZZALUNA
1821 SE 10th Ave., Fort Lauderdale: 954-522-9191
http://www.bistromezzaluna.com
CUISINE: Italian/ Seafood
DRINKS: Full Bar
SERVING: Dinner
Definitely a great place located in Fort Lauderdale's yachting district. Here you will dine among yacht crew and boat captains. The seafood is fresh, the service is good, the prices are steep. $$$$

BURLOCK COAST SEAFARE & SPIRITS
1 N Ft Lauderdale Beach Blvd, Ft Lauderdale, 954-302-6460
www.ritzcarlton.com
CUISINE: American (New)/Seafood
DRINKS: Full Bar
SERVING: Breakfast, Lunch & Dinner
PRICE RANGE: $$$
Located on the water in the swanky Ritz-Carlton, this 4-diamond eatery offers a good selection of American

cuisine. I am always suspicious when I run up against names like this. Burlock Coast Seafare? What is that? Who's Burlock? Then I read the place "channels the creativity of Prohibition Era rumrunners." Oh, please. Someone in a PR firm wrote that crap. This sophisticated place is about as far from the "creativity of Prohibition rumrunners" as you can possibly get. But I know how excellent the chef is, so I look beyond the bullshit. Though there are no real surprises on the wide-ranging menu, take heart because the food is locally sourced, the execution is beyond compare and the flavor combinations are creative. Picks: Charred octopus, Pork belly tacos; Lobster pappardelle; Roasted swordfish. Great choice for brunch (one of the busiest in town because of its great food and choice waterfront location) with dishes like Zaks Brioche French Toast Sandwich; Lake Meadow poached eggs with pork belly and more. Nice cocktail selection. Tip: check the web site for their daily specials to reduce the tab here. They have something different every day.

CAFÉ MARTORANO
3343 E. Oakland Park Blvd., Fort Lauderdale: 954-561-2554
http://www.cafemartorano.com
CUISINE: Italian
DRINKS: Full Bar
SERVING: Dinner
OK, so the kitschy, storefront location doesn't impress anyone; but the food certainly will. Loud and lively, this place serves up such good Italian fare that people will wait up to 2 hours for a table. Oh, and pay

attention to who's sitting at the table next to you; celebrities are known to stop by when in town. $$$$

CAFE VICO
1125 N Federal Hwy, Fort Lauderdale: 954-565-9681
http://www.cafevicorestaurant.com
CUISINE: Italian
DRINKS: Full Bar
SERVING: Lunch/ Dinner
Although this place is pricey, some would argue it's the best Italian food they've had, so it's worth it. The lasagna is particularly good. Come early because this place fills up quickly. Another must-have: the crème brulee. $$$$

CASA D'ANGELO
1201 N. Federal Hwy, Fort Lauderdale: 954-564-1234
http://www.casa-d-angelo.com
CUISINE: Italian
DRINKS: Full Bar
SERVING: Dinner
Tuscan style Italian food served up by friendly, knowledgeable staff. Take note: everything here is homemade and you can certainly taste it. Gnocchi is a standout, as is the steak Florentine (that you don't see very often these days), the snapper oreganata for something light but full-flavored and the fettuccine with roasted veal ragu top my list. Extensive wine list. $$$$

CHIMA BRAZILIAN STEAKHOUSE
2400 E Las Olas Blvd., Fort Lauderdale: 954-712-0580
http://chima.cc
CUISINE: Brazilian Steakhouse
DRINKS: Full Bar
SERVING: Dinner
Mediocre at best. The salad bar is not very good compared to other local steakhouses of this type. Service is not very attentive and it can be quite loud.
$$$$

DUNE
AUBERGE BEACH RESIDENCE & SPA
2200 N Ocean Blvd, 754-900-4059
https://dunefl.com
CUISINE: American (New)/Seafood
DRINKS: Full Bar

SERVING: Dinner
PRICE RANGE: $$$$
NEIGHBORHOOD: Auberge Beach
Beachfront upscale dining in a big resort. Big bar scene in a room bright with white light. There's a row of shelves behind a platoon of booths that is just filled with "stuff." Vases, pillows, trinkets, plants, knick-knacks. (who has to dust these things?) But it's very pretty, and even at night, these shelves are carefully lighted. Outside seating is plentiful, right on the water. Menu focuses on locally sourced seafood, but it has a little bit of everything. Menu picks: Yellowfin Tuna Crudo; Halibut served with crispy pancetta; Vadouvan Poached Monkfish; and Octopus a la Plancha. (several nice cuts of beef.) Beach-inspired signature cocktails. Nice wine list.

PRIME STEAK AND SEAFOOD

JWB PRIME STEAK
1111 N. Ocean Dr, Hollywood, 954-874-4470
www.jwbrestaurant.com
CUISINE: Steakhouse/Seafood
DRINKS: Full bar
SERVING: Dinner
PRICE RANGE: $$$

Steakhouse also known for its high quality seafood selection. When you spot the humongous flip-flop that signals you've arrived at Jimmy Buffet's Margaritaville, you'll know you're close to JWB, which is next door. Browse the huge raw bar that greets you when you enter. Check out the spear-caught fish-of-the-day that they claim. (I've always been skeptical that these selections were really spear-caught.) Favorites: Paella and Lobster sushi roll.

LOBSTER BAR SEA GRILLE
450 E Las Olas Blvd, Ft Lauderdale, 954-772-2675
www.buckheadrestaurants.com/lobster-bar-sea-grille
CUISINE: Seafood / Steakhouse
DRINKS: Full Bar
SERVING: Dinner nightly, Lunch weekdays
PRICE RANGE: $$$$

Modern-contemporary eatery (glistening white marble bar-top; waiters in white shirts & black vests; an oyster-appetizer kitchen in the middle of the dining room) with a creative menu of seafood and steaks. Menu favorites include: Local Snapper and Wild New

Zealand Fresh Catch. Of course, they are known for their lobster dishes. As for the side dishes, the cauliflower gratin was tasty with lots of cheese.

STEAK 954
W Hotel
401 N. Fort Lauderdale Beach Blvd., Fort Lauderdale: 954-414-8333
http://www.steak954.com
CUISINE: Steakhouse
DRINKS: Full Bar
SERVING: Breakfast/ Lunch/ Dinner
Located in the very trendy W Hotel on Ft. Lauderdale Beach, this place is every bit tasteful as it is playful. This steakhouse also has seafood, sandwiches and a raw bar on their menu. The centerpiece of the restaurant? A mesmerizing reef aquarium filled with jellyfish. Like we said, playful. $$$$

SUSHI ROCK CAFE
1515 E Las Olas Blvd., Fort Lauderdale: 954-462-5541
https://www.facebook.com/pages/Sushi-Rock-Cafe/117059118312951
CUISINE: Sushi
DRINKS: Beer/ Wine
SERVING: Dinner
Just your average sushi restaurant. The food is average, the ambience is average and parking can be a problem. You decide. $$$

VALENTINO'S CUCINA ITALIANA
620 S Federal Hwy, Fort Lauderdale: 954-523-5767

www.valentinocucinaitaliana.com
CUISINE: Italian
DRINKS: Beer / Wine
SERVING: Dinner
Amazing northern Italian cuisine. The staff is very
friendly and knowledgeable. This a great "special
occasion" restaurant. They have a great wine list but
if you're not too familiar with Italian wines, the staff
here will guide you to make the perfect selection.
$$$$

WILD SEA OYSTER BAR & GRILLE
620 E Las Olas Blvd, Ft Lauderdale, 954-467-2555
www.wildsealasolas.com
CUISINE: Seafood / Steakhouse
DRINKS: Full Bar
SERVING: Dinner nightly
PRICE RANGE: $$$
Located at the **Riverside Hotel**, this upscale seafood
eatery offers an impressive menu of items like
swordfish, grouper, wreckfish. Raw bar and wine list
featuring more than 200 labels. There's also a
delicious beef tenderloin with mushroom madeira jus.
Late-night lounge vibe.

MODERATE

ASIA BAY
1111 E Las Olas Blvd., Fort Lauderdale: 954-848-9900
http://www.asiabayrestaurants.com
CUISINE: Sushi/ Japanese/ Thai
DRINKS: Beer/ Wine
SERVING: Lunch/ Dinner
Cute restaurant with an option to sit by the water. The sushi is excellent and the chef gets very creative with the Thai dishes. $$$

THE BALCONY
1309 E Las Olas Blvd, 754-200-6344
https://thebalconylasolas.com
CUISINE: American
DRINKS: Full Bar
SERVING: Lunch, Dinner

PRICE RANGE: $$
NEIGHBORHOOD: Las Olas
Always packed 2-level eatery with an open-air
rooftop and balcony bar. Has a very busy bar scene
with lots of TV monitors above the bars. They lower
the lights at night, so it's not that bright. Live music
most nights. Colorful tiled steps lead the way up to
the second-level balcony bar, where it's just as busy.
American fare and gussied-up bar grub such as
Bangers 'n Mash; Fish 'n Chips; Mac & Cheese
Balls; Steamed Mussels; Flatbreads; Reuben Spring
Rolls. There are a few salads for those who don't
want this kind of food. Craft cocktails. Reservations
recommended.

BILLY'S STONE CRAB
400 N. Ocean Dr, Hollywood, 954-923-2300
www.crabs.com
CUISINE: Seafood
DRINKS: Full bar
SERVING: Lunch/Dinner
PRICE RANGE: $$$
Popular eatery for several decades offering a wide
variety of fresh seafood including fresh stone crabs,
lobster tails, King Crab legs, mahi-mahi, grouper,
snapper, and Norwegian Salmon. Seating inside and
out by the water on the Intracoastal. Upstairs it's a
good deal fancier and you can expect a fine dining
experience. Downstairs it's ultra casual. They offer a
different "all-you-can-eat" dinner 7 nights a week
that's a bargain.

BLUE MOON FISH CO.
4405 W. Tradewinds Ave, Lauderdale by the Sea,
954-267-9888
www.bluemoonfishco.com
CUISINE: Seafood
DRINKS: Full bar
SERVING: Lunch/Dinner
PRICE RANGE: $$$
Bright and spacious eatery overlooking the
Intracoastal Waterway serves up food from an
impressive menu. They cover all the bases here, and
that might explain why they've been in business so
long. They have a great happy hour. They have a
great raw bar selection. They have a great weekend
brunch. They have a great water view. They have
wine dinners. They have a friendly staff. Menu picks:
Fish Ceviche & Conch and Lump Crab and Roasted
Corn Black Grouper. Dessert lovers should order the
Icky Sticky (white chocolate bread pudding with
junky monkey ice cream).

BOATYARD

1555 SE 17th St, Fort Lauderdale, 954-525-7400
www.boatyard.restaurant
CUISINE: Seafood
DRINKS: Full bar
SERVING: Lunch & Dinner daily
PRICE RANGE: $$$

Expansive restaurant with indoor and outdoor service overlooking the water. Relaxed Florida nautical-themed eatery that's a great date night pick featuring an open kitchen and raw bar cart. But lunch is just as good an option because you get great daytime views of the Intracoastal. Menu of fresh seafood. Menu favorites: St. Bart's Ceviche and Fresh Grouper. Happy hour specials. The food here is good, not great, just good. Stick to the fish, it's fresh. Their daily soup, a seafood chowder, seems like everything that was left over from the night before was thrown into a pot and cooked. (And I'm not saying that's a bad thing, but a good thing.) Those of you old enough will remember the Bimini Boatyard. This is the same location spruced up quite nicely. The food is superlative compared to those bygone days of fried fish platters and other crap. You'll love this place.

BOKAMPERS SPORTS BAR & GRILL
BO'S BAR

3115 NE 32 Ave, Fort Lauderdale, 954-900-5584
https://bokampers.com/fort-lauderdale/
CUISINE: American Traditional
DRINKS: Full Bar
SERVING: Lunch, Dinner, Brunch
PRICE RANGE: $$

NEIGHBORHOOD: Los Olas

A sprawling restaurant with one of those "something-for-everyone" menus that goes on for pages. Best thing about the place is that it's right on the Intracoastal Waterway. Weekends is a bit tiresome because it's so crowded. (I've been here several times on our boat, so I know this to be true.) Best time I find to be here is early, just when they open. But if this is the scene you want, it doesn't really matter. There are so many tables it's hard not to get a good view of the water, unless you sit at the bar inside and face the TV monitors showing sports. Typical American fare such as Spinach & Artichoke Dip; Loaded Nachos (and boy, are they loaded!); Bo's Sliders (blue cheese, onions, bacon marmalade); Guacamole; Flatbreads; Wings; Burgers (with some clever twists, none of them calorie-conscious). Lots of sandwiches; Tacos; sushi. See what I mean? They have it all. There's an appetizer that sets the tone for this menu: Bo's Sampler (Southwest chicken eggrolls, onions rings, mozzarella sticks and chicken tenders). Makes me ill to think about it, but when you order something like that, thinking seldom enters the equation. Good salads for the sane among you. Still, no matter what they serve, it's a great place to take in the boat traffic.

BOMBAY DARBAR
1521 E Las Olas Blvd, 954-990-7222
www.bombaydarbar.com
CUISINE: Indian/Asian Fusion
DRINKS: Full Bar
SERVING: Lunch, Dinner

PRICE RANGE: $$
NEIGHBORHOOD: Las Olas
Big & busy Indian eatery with a weird purple-blue
lighting scheme that I find a little off-putting, but it's
no big deal. White tablecloth service with huge
crystal chandeliers as highlights in the main room. A
very large bar area, featuring the usual array of TV
monitors one expects in most Lauderdale restaurants,
no matter the cuisine or the level of service. Has a
menu featuring Indian and Asian fare, such as
Basmati Rice specialties (with chicken, lamb or
shrimp); Shrimp Goan Curry; and Lamb Chop
Masala. Lots of chicken preparations and a half dozen
lamb dishes. Clay oven dishes, Naan/Roti, it goes on
and on. A wealth of Vegetarian options.

CAFE SEVILLE
2768 E Oakland Park Blvd., Fort Lauderdale: 954-
565-1148
http://www.cafeseville.com
CUISINE: Spanish

DRINKS: Beer/ Wine
SERVING: Dinner
Small and charming, the people here really know what they are doing. Absolutely everything on the menu is delicious. Check out the daily specials, sometimes they have rabbit. The staff is very friendly and don't be surprised if the owner stops by your table to say hello. You will not be disappointed. $$$

CANYON RESTAURANT
1818 E Sunrise Blvd., Fort Lauderdale: 954-765-1950
http://www.canyonfl.com
CUISINE: American
DRINKS: Full Bar
SERVING: Dinner
Quiet and cozy, this place does not take reservations. On the weekends there will be a wait. Excellent food . Must haves: prickly pear margarita and the bread pudding. $$$

CAP'S PLACE
2765 NE 28th Ct, Lighthouse Point, 954-941-0418
www.capsplace.com
CUISINE: Seafood
DRINKS: Full Bar
SERVING: Dinner nightly except Monday, when they are closed.
PRICE RANGE: $$$
They've been dishing up fresh caught fish in this odd location since 1930. Everybody who's been in Florida for a long time has probably been to Cap's Place. If you haven't, definitely put it on your bucket list. To get here, you have to drive through a residential

section of Lighthouse Point to get to a wharf where you hop aboard a 25-foot long boat that transports you across Lake Placid to the ramshackle restaurant that looks like they haven't touched it since President Roosevelt ate here with Winston Churchill in the 1940s. This landmark eatery offers a great menu featuring seafood favorites like dolphin, wahoo, cobia, snapper, lobster and stone crab. (The crab cake starter is among the best I've ever had and the bacon-wrapped scallops are really good.) After visiting this place, you'll definitely tell your friends about it. Free parking at the wharf.

CARLOS & PEPE'S 17TH ST CANTINA
1302 SE 17th St., Fort Lauderdale: 954-467-8335
http://www.carlosandpepesfl.com
CUISINE: Tex Mex
DRINKS: Full Bar
SERVING: Dinner
If you like Tex Mex, you will probably like this place. The service is a little slow and the staff is not very friendly, except for the bartenders. It's best to sit at the bar and eat. $$$

CASA D'ANGELO RISTORANTE
1201 N Federal Hwy, Fort Lauderdale: 954-564-1234
http://www.casa-d-angelo.com
CUISINE: Italian
DRINKS: Full Bar
SERVING: Dinner
Very good Italian food in a comfortable setting. The bar area is a little small. The food is exceptional, it's

very difficult to find good Italian food but this place makes it. The wine list is extensive. $$$

CASA SENSEI
1200 E Las Olas Blvd, 954-530-4176
www.casasensei.com
CUISINE: Pan Asian / Latin American Fusion
DRINKS: Full Bar
SERVING: Lunch & Dinner -Wed-Sun, Dinner only on Mon & Tues.
PRICE RANGE: $$
NEIGHBORHOOD: Las Olas
Waterfront eatery that has to be one of the nicest interiors to be found in Lauderdale (which is not exactly a design Mecca). The dripping splotches of color (like balloons or flowers) dominating the wall treatment are lovely. Or sit outside overlooking a canal, which is very nice. The menu offers an almost scary combination of Asian dishes mashed up with Latin influences. I am always skeptical when confronted with these hodgepodge menus, but there's no disputing the flavorful food served here. It's impressive. Favorites: Mongolian Duck; China sticky ribs; Argentine Empanadas; Cuban Tostones; Honey Walnut Shrimp; Burnt fish roll. Lots of fresh seafood & veggie selections. Tropical desserts.

CASABLANCA CAFE
3049 Alhambra St., Fort Lauderdale: 954-764-3500
http://www.casablancacafeonline.com
CUISINE: Mediterranean
DRINKS: Full Bar
SERVING: Lunch/ Dinner
What makes this place great is their location. Situated
in a Spanish style building right across from the
ocean, here you will enjoy both the views and the
passersby. The food is just OK and the service is hit
or miss. $$$

CHRISTINA WAN'S MANDARIN HOUSE
664 N Federal Hwy, Fort Lauderdale: 954-527-0228
http://www.christinawans.com
CUISINE: Chinese
DRINKS: Beer/ Wine
SERVING: Lunch/ Dinner
Really, really good Chinese food and reasonably
priced. Christina is usually right there to great you as

you come in. Comfy booths and tables make this a must-visit if you're up for Chinese. $$

COOPER'S HAWK
The Galleria at Fort Lauderdale
2568 E Sunrise Blvd, 754-55-9463
www.chwinery.com
CUISINE: American (New)
DRINKS: Full Bar
SERVING: Lunch, Dinner
PRICE RANGE: $$
NEIGHBORHOOD: Coconut Creek
A wine store that also has a restaurant—so some people come just to sample the wines, and they have a large selection by the glass. I love this place because the things they do are done very well. The wine part of the operation is beyond excellent. And the menu? The menu is quite impressive. My favorites: Sweet & Crunchy Shrimp; Chopped Deviled Eggs & Toast; Meatballs in tomato sauce served with Polenta crostini (this is so good, you'll send the watier back for more); several flatbreads; Pan-roasted barramundi; Chicken parmesan; Crispy Asian Pork (potatoes with Wasabi butter, Asian slaw, pickled cucumber—outstanding). Impressive wine flights.

DOWNTOWNER
10 S. New River Dr. E., Fort Lauderdale: 954-463-9800
www.downtownersaloon.com
CUISINE: American; sports bar pub food
DRINKS: Full Bar
SERVING: Brunch/ Lunch/ Dinner/ Late Night

It's a little hard to describe this place, the food is really good and you can catch your favorite team on any of the many flat screens. Each night is a different specialty: Mondays is steak night, Tuesday is ribs night… you get the picture. Particularly good is the all-you-can-eat crab legs on Sunday nights. $$

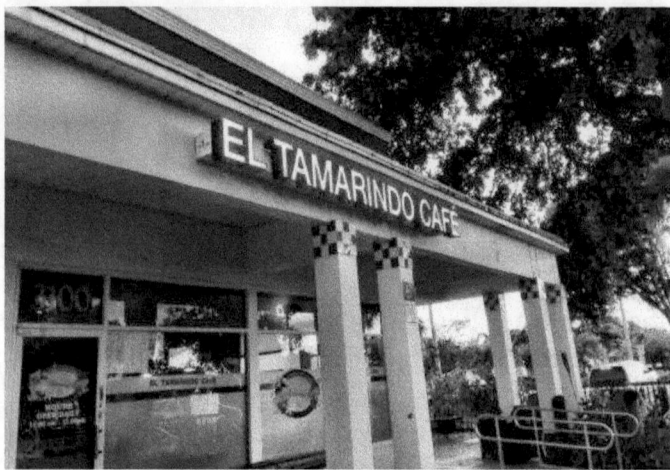

EL TAMARINDO CAFÉ
233 W. State Road 84, Fort Lauderdale: 954-467-5114
www.eltamarindocafe.com
CUISINE: Salvadorean/ Latin
DRINKS: Full Bar
SERVING: Breakfast/ Lunch/ Dinner
Who would think that the best Salvadorean food would be in Fort Lauderdale? This place serves traditional favorites like *pupusas* (corn tortillas stuffed with pork, beans, cheese or mixed), hearty beef soup, or *tamal de elote* (a delicious sweet corn tamale). White tablecloths and cheery, courteous

service combine to make this a magnate for Latin food lovers. $$

EDUARDO DE SAN ANGEL
2822 E. Commercial Blvd, Fort Lauderdale: 954-772-4731
http://www.eduardodesanangel.com
CUISINE: Mexican
DRINKS: Beer/ Wine
SERVING: Lunch/ Dinner
Gourmet Mexican food at its best. This is not Mexican like you're used to, it's better. From their *jaibas rellenas* (stuffed Florida blue crab) to the ancho chile flavored crepe. Oh and yes, here you will also find *mole poblano*, a Mexican favorite. $$$

GILBERT'S 17TH STREET GRILL
1821 Cordova Rd., Fort Lauderdale: 954-768-8990
http://www.gilberts17thstgrill.com
CUISINE: American
DRINKS: Beer/ Wine
SERVING: Lunch/ Dinner
Now this is the place to go if you want a REALLY good burger. One of the best in town. The food is really fresh and cooked to order. All the soups are home made. Really good service. $$

GREEK ISLANDS TAVERNA
3300 N Ocean Blvd., Fort Lauderdale: 954-565-5505
http://www.greekislandstaverna.com
CUISINE: Greek/ Mediterranean
DRINKS: Full Bar
SERVING: Lunch/ Dinner
Everything on the menu here is excellent. Specialties
include the lamb chops, hummus and pita bread and
grilled octopus. The environment is typically Greek,
loud and welcoming. $$$

HENRY'S SANDWICH STATION
FATVillage
545 NW 1st Ave, Ft Lauderdale, 954-616-5538
www.henryssandwich.com
CUISINE: Sandwiches

DRINKS: Beer & Wine Only
SERVING: Breakfast, Lunch & Dinner, Brunch only
on Sundays.
PRICE RANGE: $$
Popular eatery in FATVillage. Big overstuffed
sandwiches beautifully crafted. Expect a line at peak
times. Favorites: "Montreal style" smoked brisket on
Zak the Baker's rye; Fried chicken sandwich; Pork
shoulder and ham sandwich. Amazing key lime pie.
Outdoor patio dining available.

INDIGO
Riverside Hotel
620 E. Las Olas Blvd., Fort Lauderdale: 954-467-
0671
www.riversidehotel.com
CUISINE: Seafood/ American
DRINKS: Full Bar
SERVING: Breakfast/ Lunch/ Dinner
Located in the lobby of the historic **Riverside Hotel**,
here you can dine and watch the endless parade of
people that promenade along Las Olas Boulevard.
Menu highlights include a char-grilled pork loin and a
citrus crusted Florida grouper. $$-$$$

J. MARK'S RESTAURANT & BAR
1245 N Federal Hwy, Fort Lauderdale: 954-390-0770
http://www.jmarksrestaurant.com
CUISINE: American
DRINKS: Full Bar
SERVING: Lunch/ Dinner/ Brunch on weekends
Popular and upscale eatery, this place is usually busy
and once you've had the food, you'll understand why.

One of the best things on the menu: the Chilean Sea Bass that literally melts in your mouth. Crab cakes are also quite good. Very friendly staff. $$-$$$

KELLY'S LANDING
1305 SE 17th St., Ft Lauderdale: 954-760-7009
www.kellyslanding.com
CUISINE: American/ Seafood
DRINKS: Full Bar
SERVING: Lunch/ Dinner
Snowbirds searching for the flavors of home while visiting Florida will find what they're looking for at Kelly's Landing. They import lobsters daily from Boston and serve up a popular New England-style seafood and clam chowder. $$

KURO
1 Seminole Way, Hollywood, 954-327-7625
www.seminolehardrockhollywood.com
CUISINE: Sushi/Japanese
DRINKS: Full bar
SERVING: Dinner; Lunch on Saturdays
PRICE RANGE: $$$
Spacious modern eatery set inside the Seminole Hard Rock Casino. Fresh sushi and unique crafted cocktails. Menu favorites: Tuna Crispy Rice and Wagyu Tacos.

LA BAMBA
4245 N Federal Hwy, Fort Lauderdale: 954-568-5662
http://www.labamba123.com
CUISINE: Mexican
DRINKS: Full Bar

SERVING: Lunch/ Dinner
If you know true Mexican food, you will know that this is standardized American-Mexican food. In other words, not very good. Service is adequate but the place can get really loud. $$

LAS VEGAS CUBAN CUISINE
2807 E Oakland Park Blvd., Fort Lauderdale: 954-564-1370
http://www.lasvegascubancuisine.com
CUISINE: Cuban
DRINKS: Full Bar
SERVING: Lunch/ Dinner
Very simple menu, all the Cuban basics. Good service and reasonable prices. Crowded for lunch. $$

LONA COCINA TEQUILERIA
The Westin
321 N Fort Lauderdale Beach Blvd, Ft Lauderdale, 954-245-3069
www.lonarestaurant.com
CUISINE: Mexican
DRINKS: Full Bar
SERVING: Lunch & Dinner (breakfast available in another restaurant called Tinta).
PRICE RANGE: $$
Causal Mexican eatery right on the beach has a laid back feel to it, befitting its location. Cactus planters and the color scheme give it a Santa Fe feel. Indoor-outdoor bar serves up some great margaritas, and they don't use the crappy tequilas other joints serve the idiot drunken Spring Breakers. Menu offers a wide range of traditional Mexican dishes, from starters like

Tortilla soup, but also has some fresh twists, like a
Mexican chopped salad (with Romaine, bacon,
roasted corn, cherry tomatoes, chickpeas, queso
fresco tossed in a cilantro ranch dressing). Favorites:
Chicken enchiladas; Beef Barbacoa tacos; Carne
Asada (grilled skirt steak). Large selection of tequila.
Gluten-free options.

LOUIE BOSSI'S RISTORANTE BAR PIZZERIA
1032 E Las Olas Blvd, Fort Lauderdale, 954-356-
6699
www.louiebossi.com
CUISINE: Italian
DRINKS: Full Bar
SERVING: Lunch & Dinner
PRICE RANGE: $$
NEIGHBORHOOD: Downtown
Popular eatery serving authentic Italian cuisine
including Neapolitan pies, pastas, salami and piazza
with bocce. Happy hour every day. Creative cocktails
like the pineapple martini. Nice wine list. Indoor and
outdoor seating.

MAI-KAI POLYNESIAN DINNER SHOW
3599 N. Federal Hwy, Fort Lauderdale: 954-563-3272
http://www.maikai.com
ADMISSION: Show charge: $10.95 per person plus dinner. Kids menu available.
The roaring drums mark the beginning of the exciting "island revue." It's about as phony now as it was a hundred years ago when they first came up with this concept of a "romantic Hawaiian wedding dance" and the "thrilling Samoan fire knife dance performed by our native Polynesian dancers." To read it, you want to barf. But trust me, it's a lot of fun. And the food's good, too.

MARIO'S CATALINA RESTAURANT
1611 N Federal Hwy, Fort Lauderdale: 954-563-4141
www.catalinarestaurant.net

CUISINE: Cuban/ Spanish
DRINKS: Beer/ Wine
SERVING: Lunch/ Dinner
Lively little restaurant with great beef empanadas and
Argentine style skirt steak. Another must-have is the
seafood-replete paella. The staff is warm and friendly.
$$

MOJO
4140 N Federal Hwy, Fort Lauderdale: 954-568-4443
http://www.mojofl.com
CUISINE: International
DRINKS: Full Bar
SERVING: Dinner
Good food being served up in a very colorful
environment. The walls are covered with art. You
won't be disappointed with anything on the menu,
and the service is fast and friendly. Cool place with a
good vibe. $$

RAINBOW PALACE
2787 E Oakland Park Blvd., Fort Lauderdale: 954-
565-5652
http://www.rainbowpalace.com
CUISINE: Chinese
DRINKS: Full Bar
SERVING: Lunch/ Dinner
Quite possibly the best Chinese food in Fort
Lauderdale. The ambiance is quite nice and the staff
is friendly. The menu is extensive. $$

RUSTIC INN CRABHOUSE
4331 Anglers Ave., Fort Lauderdale: 954-584-1637
http://www.rusticinn.com
CUISINE: Seafood
DRINKS: Full Bar
SERVING: Lunch/ Dinner
Bright and raucous, in here you have the opportunity to take a mallet and crack your own crabs! Delicious as they are in their garlicky oil sauce, trust me, you will need the bibs they provide. On the water but in an odd location, this is not the place for a quiet, romantic dinner. Although entrees will run you between $10 - $20, crabs are market price, and they can get pricey. $$-$$$

SAGE FRENCH CAFÉ AND OYSTER BAR
2378 N. Federal Hwy., Ft. Lauderdale: 954-565-2299
http://www.sagecafe.net
CUISINE: French
DRINKS: Beer/ Wine
SERVING: Lunch/ Dinner
Superb country French cuisine at reasonable prices in
a casual French bistro setting. Among their best
dishes is a *daube de boeuf* (a slow cooked beef stew)
and a *saumon coulibiac* (salmon baked in a puff
pastry). Their wine list includes both French and
domestic. $$

SAPIDO RESTAURANT & CAFÉ
111 SE 8th Ave, 954-488-8000
www.sapidocafe.com
CUISINE: Italian
DRINKS: Beer & Wine
SERVING: Lunch & Dinner – Mon – Fri, Dinner
only on Sat & Sun.
PRICE RANGE: $$
NEIGHBORHOOD: Las Olas
Casual eatery with bare bones tables & chairs,
nothing fancy. Against dark walls, they've placed
shelves holding lots of bottles of wine and other
things used every day, like glassware and plates and
bags of coffee. This creates a very cozy feeling. They
offer a creative menu of Italian fare, with the pasta
being homemade here on site. Favorites: Ravioli with
Lobster; Gnocchi al Pesto; Octopus salad; Lasagna
alla Bolognese (this melts in your mouth); Bruschetta
and Taglieri. Daily specials. Nice selection of Italian
wines.

SEASONS 52
2428 E Sunrise Blvd. (inside Galleria Mall), Fort
Lauderdale: 954-537-1052
http://www.seasons52.com
CUISINE: American
DRINKS: Full Bar
SERVING: Lunch/ Dinner
While the décor here is somewhat dark and moody,
it's always very lively. This place is great for an
intimate dinner. The food is great and the service is
also very good. You'll be surprised to know that
everything on the menu is under 450 calories and they

change it with the seasons. There's a HUGE bar, which is where I like to eat if I'm with just one other person. $$

SECRET GARDEN
THE PILLARS
111 N. Birch Rd., Fort Lauderdale: 954-467-9639
www.pillarshotel.com
This is the very nice restaurant in the posh and exclusive Pillars just off the Beach. They serve breakfast and lunch to hotel guests only, but at dinner they let members of the Secret Garden Society in. Chef Hammi combines fresh food with interesting cross-cultural ingredients and elegant presentations. His clean and bright flavors reflect the influences of a Moroccan heritage and techniques absorbed while working under top chefs in some of New York City's greatest kitchens. (Call or email them at

secretgarden@pillarshotel.com to see if they'll let you squeeze in for dinner.)

STEELPAN KITCHEN & BAR
SONESTA
999 N Fort Lauderdale Beach Blvd, 954-302-5252
www.steelpanftl.com
CUISINE: Caribbean/Seafood
DRINKS: Full bar
SERVING: Breakfast, Lunch, Dinner
PRICE RANGE: $$
NEIGHBORHOOD: Central Beach
Caribbean inspired eatery that has a bright & cheery ambience offers an extensive seafood focused menu. The dishes are elegantly prepared and beautiful to look at, especially the whole baked snapper. Favorites: Sesame Seared Tuna; Caribbean Jerk Wings; Crab & Corn Chowder; Jerk Chicken with potato dumplings; Braised short ribs with Peruvian garlic potatoes; the Steelpan Burger comes with Bermuda onions and smoked bacon jam. Because this place is in the Sonesta, they offer breakfast, and it's a full breakfast menu, and very satisfying & reasonable, from the hot flaky croissants to the 3-egg omelet to the French toast with a Caribbean twist with cream cheese, guava and topped with a dusting of cinnamon. Yum.

SWEET NECTAR CHARCOAL GRILL AND SPIRITS
1017 E Las Olas Blvd, Ft Lauderdale, 954-761-2122
www.sweetnectarbuzz.com
CUISINE: American (New) / Tapas / Small Plates

DRINKS: Full Bar
SERVING: Lunch & Dinner
PRICE RANGE: $$
Casual neighborhood spot with a menu of American small plates. A favorite of locals who keep coming back for the classic cuisine and handcrafted cocktails. (At happy hour, those expensive craft cocktails cost 50% less.) Only 30 people can squeeze into the interior, but they can handle about 100 outside, so if it's summer, make sure you're inside. The whole snapper is char-grilled, so that's the best option. The Brussels sprouts are roasted in a skillet and topped with a kimchi vinaigrette that gives them a pleasant bite.

TERRA MARE
551 N Fort Lauderdale Beach Blvd, Ft Lauderdale, 954-414-5160
www.terramarefl.com
CUISINE: Seafood/Tapas
DRINKS: Full Bar
SERVING: Breakfast, Lunch & Dinner
PRICE RANGE: $$$
Located in the **Conrad Hotel**, right across from the ocean, this swanky eatery has an impressive menu and the design is modern without being too fussy. By all means try to get a table out on the porch so you have a good view of the water. ("Terra Mare" means "land and sea" in Italian.) They pride themselves on sourcing ingredients locally when possible. A little pricier than you normally expect in Lauderdale, but that's not a bad thing, since the food is heads and shoulders above most other places. Favorites: Spiced

duck breast with curried lentils; Grilled romaine (with anchovies, avocado, Parmesan); Seared scallops (with jalapeno-corn "sponge"); get a side order of the truffled grits au jus; Creative desserts.

THE TERRACE GRILL
THE DALMAR HOTEL
299 N Federal Hwy, 954-945-9300
www.theterracegrill.com
CUISINE: American (New)
DRINKS: Full Bar
SERVING: Dinner, Closed Mondays
PRICE RANGE: $$
NEIGHBORHOOD:
The upscale Dalmar is the setting for this stylish supper club with a capacious bar where they use the bottle rack above the bar as a design element. It works. Very pretty, high-ccilinged room that has a touch of elegance. offering an impressive menu of American fare. Favorites: Dover sole; Rosemary Braised Lentils; Kurobuta Pork Chop (with charred broccolini); Lobster Bearnaise; and Fresh Idaho Trout. Classic cocktails. By the way, there's a rooftop eatery in the Dalmar that's very nice (from 5:30). It's called the **Sparrow**, and the menu is a little on the lighter side. Spectacular views of Lauderdale from up here. The inside bar is cozy and upbeat. Great design work here. Food & drinks, tops.

TIMPANO
450 E Las Olas Blvd., Fort Lauderdale: 954-462-9119
http://www.timpanochophouse.net
CUISINE: Steakhouse/ Italian

DRINKS: Full Bar
SERVING: Lunch/ Dinner
Stylish and trendy, there are always pretty people in this place. A must have is their Black Skillet Mussels. But the steaks are as good as the pasta dishes. $$

WILD SEA OYSTER BAR & GRILLE
620 E Las Olas Blvd, Fort Lauderdale, 954-467-2555
www.wildsealasolas.com
CUISINE: Seafood/Steakhouse
DRINKS: Full bar
SERVING: Dinner nightly
PRICE RANGE: $$$
Upscale seafood eatery specializing in fresh oysters. Menu favorites: Crab cakes and Po' Boy Sliders. Great selection of wines.

THE WILDER
701 E Broward Blvd, Ft Lauderdale, 954-683-9453
www.intothewilder.com
CUISINE: Lounge
DRINKS: Full Bar
SERVING: Dinner (opens at 4 pm till late)
PRICE RANGE: $$
Just a few minutes west of the beach is this chic bar and restaurant, with the emphasis purely on the bar. I have to mention it because it's such a cool, welcoming place. You'll love the wooden arched theme running through the place, the wonderful outdoor terrace at tree-level surrounded by seagrape trees; the whimsical wallpaper with palm fronds creeping along the wall like tentacles. The craft cocktails and beer selection are the main features

here. (Get the Negroni.) Very limited menu of small bites like Hearts of Palm tacos; Short rib poutine; Braised octopus; Avocado toast. Free parking behind the building. Or skip eating here. Come before dinner to scope out the place during happy hour and then come back later when it gets really busy.

INEXPENSIVE

ANTHONY'S COAL FIRED PIZZA
2203 S Federal Hwy, Fort Lauderdale: 954-462-5555
http://anthonyscoalfiredpizza.com
CUISINE: Pizza/ Italian
DRINKS: Beer/ Wine
SERVING: Lunch/ Dinner
Just really good pizza. You'll love the slightly blackened crust. Also good here are the chicken wings but for those seeking more traditional Italian dishes, they also have a selection of pasta dishes that are sure to please. $

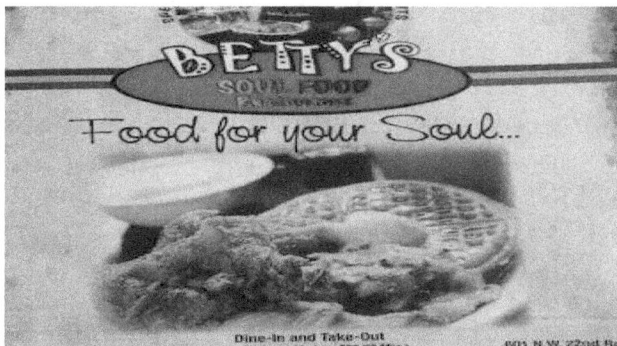

BETTY'S SOUL FOOD RESTAURANT
601 NW 22nd Rd., Fort Lauderdale: 954-583-9121

http://www.allmenus.com/fl/fort-lauderdale/15970-bettys-soul-food-restaurant/menu/
CUISINE: Southern Soul Food
DRINKS: No Alcohol
SERVING: Breakfast/ Lunch/ Dinner
This is the place to get Southern soul food. The menu is not too reliable so ask the waiter what the chef has going on. Typical items being served up: pig tails, catfish, fried chicken, chitlins, oxtail and collard greens. Always a mix of people here. $

BOMBAY CAFE
3060 N Andrews Ave., Wilton Manors: 954-568-0600
http://www.bombay-cafe.com
CUISINE: Indian
DRINKS: Beer/ Wine
SERVING: Lunch/ Dinner
Best Indian food in Broward County. The place doesn't look like much, but who cares? When you're having this kind of great food, nothing else matters. They have a great Wednesday night buffet. $

CASA FRIDA
5441 N Federal Hwy, Ft Lauderdale, 954-530-3668
www.casafridamexicancuisine.com
CUISINE: Mexican / Spanish
DRINKS: Beer & Wine only
SERVING: Lunch & Dinner; closed Mon
PRICE RANGE: $$
Inspired by the famous painter – Frida Kahlo, this colorful eatery features cuisine from a variety of regions of Mexico, all homemade and inspired by the

recipes of the owners' ancestors. On the menu is a line that reads, "There's Mexican food and there's the food of Mexico." This place serves the latter, so don't expect to come here to eat a chimichanga. LOL. Chiles rellenos, enchiladas Frida (stuffed with chicken and roasted tomatillo sauce on top) and a slow-roasted pork dish, Cochinita Pibil, which is marinated in achiote citrus juice, are good bets.

EGG N YOU DINER
2621 N Federal Hwy, Fort Lauderdale: 954-564-2045
CUISINE: American/ Diner
DRINKS: No Alcohol
SERVING: Breakfast/ Lunch
Typical greasy spoon that doesn't disappoint. Service may be a little slow and there is usually a wait for breakfast on the weekends. $

THE FLORIDIAN RESTAURANT
1410 E. Las Olas Blvd., Fort Lauderdale: 954-463-4041
www.thefloridiandiner.com
CUISINE: American/ Diner

DRINKS: Beer/ Wine
SERVING: Open 24 hours
This greasy spoon has been around for many years,
63 to be precise. A favorite among locals, this place is
packed during the weekend. Great place for breakfast
serving up oversized omelets, hot oatmeal, and
biscuits and gravy. $

FRESH FIRST
1637 SE 17ᵗʰ St, Ft Lauderdale, 954-763-3344
www.freshfirst.com
CUISINE: Gluten-free / Smoothies
DRINKS: Beer & Wine Only (even the beer and wine
are gluten-free)
SERVING: Breakfast & Lunch; closed Sun
PRICE RANGE: $$
South Florida's first 100% gluten-free eatery and
juicery serving a creative menu using fresh
ingredients and superfoods. Great spot for a healthy
breakfast or lunch. There are 3 excellent burgers:
portabello, raw lentil and quinoa veggie. Or get for
one of their creative and tasty bowls; zucchini
puttanesca (with garbanzo beans, lentils, red peppers,
scallions, Kalamata olives, basil in a garlic-lemon
sauce); or the bowl with veggie fried quinoa (with
scallions, red peppers, carrots, purple cabbage and a
fried egg on top).

THE HUMMUS HOUSE
900 NE 20th Ave, Ft Lauderdale, 954-314-7686
www.thehummushouseftl.com
CUISINE: Vegetarian/Vegan/Mediterranean/Israeli
DRINKS: No Booze

SERVING: Lunch & Dinner
PRICE RANGE: $$
NEIGHBORHOOD: Victoria Park
This place is a kind of homage to the "hummusias" you can see every couple of blocks in Israel. Authentic hummus and falafel with a variety of vegetarian and vegan dishes. "Meatless and proud" is their motto here. Traditional dishes using chicken or beef are replaced with soy, but in most cases, you couldn't even tell. Wide variety of Hummus Bowls. I liked the BBQ "chicken," but of course it wasn't really chicken. Greek salads are large. Try the Frozen Limonana, a frozen concoction with mint and ginger popular in Israel.

JACK'S OLD FASHION HAMBURGER HOUSE
4201 N Federal Hwy, Fort Lauderdale: 954-565-9960

www.jacksoldfashionhamburgers.com
CUISINE: American
DRINKS: No Alcohol
SERVING: Lunch/ Dinner
This is the place to go if you want a no frills, basic
hamburger or cheeseburger. They do charge you extra
for lettuce and tomato. They also have hot dogs and a
few sandwiches. $

LA SPADA'S ORIGINAL HOAGIES
233-B East Commercial Blvd, Lauderdale-by-the-
Sea: 954-776-7893
http://www.laspadashoagies.com
CUISINE: Sandwiches
DRINKS: No Alcohol
SERVING: Lunch/ Dinner
Whether you call it a sub or a hoagie, this place has
the best around. Fresh meats and veggies piled high
on fresh bread makes them simply delicious! $

LE PATIO
2401 NE 11th Ave., Wilton Manors: 954-530-4641
http://www.lepatiowiltonmanors.com
CUISINE: International/ Comfort Foods
DRINKS: Beer/ Wine
SERVING: Lunch/ Dinner
YIKES! What a great place this is. You definitely
want to sit in the back patio. It's a very cute and
charming bistro atmosphere. The food is absolutely
stupendous. Favorites include the French Onion soup
and the homemade lasagna.

LESTER'S DINER

250 W State Road 84, Fort Lauderdale: 954-525-5641
www.lestersdiner.com
CUISINE: American Diner
DRINKS: Beer/ Wine
SERVING: Breakfast/ Lunch/ Dinner
Typical American diner, you will absolutely love this
place. Sit at the bar or sit in a booth, the wait staff
will take very good care of you. All the typical dishes
you will find here and the desserts are decadent. $

PIRATE REPUBLIC SEAFOOD & GRILL

400 SW 3rd Ave, Fort Lauderdale, 954-761-3500
www.piraterepublicbar.com
CUISINE: Seafood / Brazilian
DRINKS: Full bar
SERVING: Lunch/Dinner
PRICE RANGE: $$
Waterfront restaurant on the river with a pirate theme.
Menu picks: Fresh oysters, coconut shrimp, whole
fried snapper, shrimp Alfredo. There are some nice

dishes you won't see just anywhere—the Pirate Bowl (with clams, calamari, shrimp, mussels in a broth full of flavors from garlic, butter and white wine) and Brazilian seafood moqueca (a mix of lobster and octopus in a great sauce). Great view from the deck. Their Key Lime Pie is a must.

PIZZA CITY
1509 E Las Olas Blvd., Fort Lauderdale: 954-523-1313
www.pizzacityitalian.com
CUISINE: Pizza
DRINKS: Beer/ Wine
SERVING: Lunch/ Dinner
Basic fare pizza, pasta, subs and calzones. They offer gluten-free pizza crust. $$

PIZZACRAFT ARTISAN PIZZERIA
330 Himmarshee St Ste 101, Fort Lauderdale, 954-616-8028
www.pizzacraftpizzeria.com
CUISINE: Pizza/Italian
DRINKS: Full bar
SERVING: Lunch & Dinner
PRICE RANGE: $$
Creative menu of pizza and typical Italian fare. Here you'll be treated to wood fired pizzas (meatball pizza is a favorite). Don't overlook the variety of house made pastas. Half-price specials on Wednesdays. Nice bar selection.

PRESS GOURMET SANDWICHES
6206 N Federal Hwy, Fort Lauderdale, 954-440-0422

www.pressgourmetsandwiches.com
CUISINE: Sandwiches
DRINKS: No Booze
SERVING: Lunch & Dinner
PRICE RANGE: $
NEIGHBORHOOD: East side of US 1

Basically a sandwich shop (with a clever newspaper theme) serving gourmet sandwiches and sides like Truffle Fries and Mac'n Cheese Balls. A couple of culinary stars that had a food truck decided to open a permanent location, and this is it. Simply wonderful food prepared with top-notch ingredients (that you'd expect from graduates of the culinary school Johnson & Wales) and the portions are huge. The "Sentinel" is a cheesesteak sandwich with caramelized onions that melts in your mouth. The "Journal" is a pork lover's delight—pulled pork delectably flavored with a sweet tangy BBQ sauce, coleslaw and onion straws that are crispy and delightful. (You can order the onion straws on the side, which I definitely recommend—you will want more of them.) Order and pay at the counter. Weekly specials.

RIVERSIDE MARKET SOUTH
3218 SE 6th Ave, Fort Lauderdale, 954-524-8986
www.theriversidemarket.com
CUISINE: Gastropub
DRINKS: Beer & Wine Only
SERVING: Lunch & Dinner; Closed Sun
PRICE RANGE: $$
NEIGHBORHOOD: Btwn the Sailboat Bend and Riverside Park

Great selection of food including their famous flat bread pizzas. Menu picks: Shrimp Po Boy, pulled pork sandwich, mahi tacos, turkey meatball sliders and pork tacos. The desserts from nearby Pies in a Jar are worth your attention—served in chilled mason jars, you can get things like Key Lime Goodness, Chocolate Mousse Pie and other really nice selections. What's really impressive is the 32 cutting edge craft draft lines and a selection of 350 bottled beers. I'm always suspicious of places that carry hundreds of varieties of bottled beer. Beer ought to be fresh and you wonder how long that quaint beer from Lithuania has been sitting in the cooler. A year? Two years. Try out some of the local beers produced in florida, like J. Wakefield in Miami, Funky Buddha Brewery in Oakland Park.

SMOKE BBQ
3351 NE 32nd St, Fort Lauderdale, 954-530-5334

www.eatbbqnow.com
CUISINE: BBQ
DRINKS: Full bar
SERVING: Lunch & Dinner; closed Monday
PRICE RANGE: $$
Authentic BBQ eatery with a varied menu. Menu favorites include: Brisket, Ribs, and Pulled Pork.

SOUTHPORT RAW BAR
1536 Cordova Rd, Ft Lauderdale, 954-525-2526
www.southportrawbar.com
CUISINE: Seafood
DRINKS: Beer & Wine
SERVING: Lunch/Dinner/Late Night
PRICE RANGE: $$
Great meeting place in business for over 40 years that's a mixture of dive bar and boat dock eatery. Great to sit out here and scarf down shellfish while looking at the water. Menu picks: Fresh raw oysters, Fried Clam strips, dolphin, excellent clam chowder and the very best conch chowder you can find in these parts. Good selection of beers. Indoor and outdoor seating.

TACOCRAFT TAQUERIA & TEQUILA BAR
204 SW 2nd St, Fort Lauderdale, 954-463-2003
www.tacocraft.com
CUISINE: Mexican
DRINKS: Full bar
SERVING: Lunch/Dinner/Late Night
PRICE RANGE: $$
This place is a locals' favorite – especially Taco Tuesday when the tacos are cheap. And they don't

limit your choice of the kind of taco you can order on Tuesday. You can order any taco on the menu and still get the low Tuesday price. The tacos are made fresh daily here in the store. Menu favorites: Short rib taco, chicken taco, blackened ahi tuna. Indoor and outdoor seating, late night and after work crowds.

TARPON RIVER BREWING
280 SW 6th St, Ft Lauderdale, 954-353-3193
www.tarponriverbrewing.com
CUISINE: Brewery
DRINKS: Beer & Wine Only
SERVING: 8 a.m. – midnight Mon - Thurs, 8 a.m. – 2 a.m. Fri & Sat, 8 a.m. – 10 a.m. Sun
PRICE RANGE: $$
Small brewery with over a dozen rotating beers on tap (and only a couple of wines). This huge place runs up to 11,000 square feet, and was a stable back in the 1920s. Big copper brewing vats form the décor, such as it is. There's an Astro-turf patio that's nice in good weather, and when doesn't Lauderdale have good weather? Simple menu of snacks like a giant pretzels (served with beer-cheese). Favorites: Beer mac & cheese and a very flavorful Cheeseburger.

TOP HAT DELICATESSEN
415 NE 3rd St, Fort Lauderdale, 954-900-3896
www.tophatftl.com
CUISINE: Deli
DRINKS: Full bar
SERVING: Breakfast & Lunch
PRICE RANGE: $$

Modern twist on a New York Deli feature traditional deli fare like cheese blintzes, lox, sandwiches and non-deli items like ramen and crafted cocktails. Menu favorites include: Noodle Kugel and Rueben Egg Rolls. Crafted cocktails and beer.

TARKS OF DANIA BEACH
1317 S Federal Hwy, Dania Beach, 954-925-8275
https://tarks.business.site
CUISINE: Sandwiches/Bar Grub
DRINKS: Full bar
SERVING: Lunch/Dinner/Late Night
PRICE RANGE: $
Dive bar with a menu of tasty eats. I've been driving up to little Dania to get the chicken wings and the steamer clams here for three decades. They're just as good today as they were then. Favorites: Conch salad

and Grilled grouper sandwich. Very busy place – no reservations. Counter service plus a few tables outside. Since 1966.

WARSAW COFFEE COMPANY
815 NE 13th St, Fort Lauderdale, 954-990-4189
www.warsawcoffee.com
CUISINE: American/Diner
DRINKS: Beer & Wine Only
SERVING: Breakfast, Lunch & Dinner
PRICE RANGE: $
Coffee shop with an extensive menu. Great selection of coffees. Nice selection of pastries and sweets. Try their famous kitchen sink cookies.

SPORTS BARS

BOKAMPER'S SPORTS BAR & GRILL
3115 NE 32nd Ave, Fort Lauderdale, 954-900-5584
www.bokampersplantation.com
They have over 55 plasma HD TVs along with 2 of South Florida's Largest HD TVs. They play every sport, every game, every event. Stop by for you watch TV.) Daily drink specials. Private parties, catering available.
lunch, dinner or just a drink and meet Kim Bokamper. Boxing, UFC, basketball, soccer, hockey, baseball, special events. (They have a Game Room where your kids can play.)

FLANIGAN'S
1479 E. Commercial Blvd., Oakland Park: 954-493-5329

www.flanigans.net

The atmosphere of the restaurant is fun, they have lively music and everyone seems to enjoy it. The pina colada is one of the best around, not too sweet and you can actually taste the alcohol. I grew up eating his baby back ribs.

LANDLUBBERS RAW BAR & GRILL
1851 N. Pine Island Rd., Plantation: 954-473-2884
www.landlubbersbarandgrill.com

Out west of Fort Lauderdale, you'll find this friendly sports bar. This place serves up big fat burgers and fresh seafood. Crab cakes which were made with a very generous portion of real lump crab meat and the burgers are well above average. All the waitresses and waiters are nice and pleasant. (I focus on the raw bar. Here you can get a dozen oysters, raw or steamed, for $11. On South Beach where I live, those very same oysters will run you $3.50 to $4 *each*.)

MCSORLEY'S BEACH PUB

837 N. Fort Lauderdale Beach Blvd., Fort
Lauderdale: 954-565-4446
www.mcsorleysftl.com
With 25 TVs you can watch any sporting event you
want. Just a great place to drink some suds and watch
the world turn. I love the rooftop bar with its killer
view of the ocean. If there are no sports on TV, you
will find this place transformed into a cool young
hangout with great music and a great ladies' night on
a Wednesday.

MILLER'S ALE HOUSE

2861 N. Federal Hwy, Fort Lauderdale: 954-565-
5747
www.millersalehouse.com
Very good place to watch sports in Ft Lauderdale.
Central location, free parking, very good service,
reasonable prices, tasty food and lots of TVs
everywhere to catch a game. The Ale House is a
decent sports bar with a good selection of beers, a
good menu, and some great food and drink specials
during the week. (It's hard to beat the $9.95 Prime
Rib or 35 Fried Shrimp on Thursdays.)

SLACKERS BAR & GRILL

995 State Road 84, Fort Lauderdale: 954-530-4758
www.slackersbarandgrill.com
They have 33 TVs to watch your favorite game on.
They even offer customers who get a table near the
wall their own TV to watch whatever you like. Hell,
you can even have a remote and change your own
channel. They show all NFL football games with
Direc TV's Sunday Ticket, all MLB, NBA, NHL and
Rugby, and also show all UFC pay-per-view events
and every Sunday they throw a NASCAR party. They
have recently added the College Football package and
the Big Ten Network.

STOUT BAR & GRILL

3419 N. Andrews Ave., Oakland Park: 754-223-5678
www.stoutbarandgrill.com
Golf, soccer, rugby, you name it, they show it. They
have 32 HDTV screens to watch while you chow
down on their traditional menu featuring some Irish

favorites. They have a flatbread with corned beef, Swiss cheese and grain mustard that's really good. $8.

QUARTERDECK
2933 E. Las Olas Blvd., Fort Lauderdale Beach: 954-525-2010
quarterdeckrestaurants.com
A neighborhood bar with solid food, ice-cold beer, good drinks, fair prices. Seafood, steaks and ribs, burgers, wings, the usual menu for this kind of place.

Chapter 4
NIGHTLIFE

THE CULTURE ROOM
3045 N. Federal Hwy, Fort Lauderdale: 954-564-1074

http://www.cultureroom.net

If you consider rock and heavy metal to be culture, visit the Culture Room and bang your head to local bands. Open nightly from 8pm to 3am.

DICEY RILEY'S

217 SW 2nd St., Fort Lauderdale: 954-522-1908
No web site
A downtown favorite for those who love a rowdy
Irish bar featuring some of the best cover bands in
Fort Lauderdale. Be prepared to stand very close to
the person next to you on the weekends and feel free
to join the crowd as they attempt to sing along with
the band. 21+ only.

BLONDIE'S SPORTS BAR

229 S Fort Lauderdale Beach Blvd, Fort Lauderdale:
954-728-9801
http://itsbetteronthebeach.com/blondies/
Serving up the "World's Longest Happy Hour (noon-
10pm) Dirty Blondes Sports Bar is a favorite amongst
locals and voted 'Best Bar to Take Out-Of-Towners'
by New Times Magazine. Whether you're looking to

take in the game day action on one of 50 flat screen TVs, soak in the sun and scenery with a bucket of beer and a burger, add a little air hockey or pop-a-shot competition to a night out with friends, or use pinball and pool as an icebreaker for a first date, Dirty Blondes casual rock-n-roll atmosphere has a little something for everyone.

EBAR / CLUB BAR 13
215 SW 2nd St., Fort Lauderdale: 305-928-3227
www.ebarclub13.com
Fort Lauderdale's only premier Latin nightclub - Salsa, Merengue, Bachata and Reggaeton mixed with freestyle Americano. Underground dance party in (2) dark RED DISTRICT tunnels - industrial and urban design.

ELBO ROOM
241 S. Fort Lauderdale Blvd, Fort Lauderdale 954-463-4615
http://www.elboroom.com
Formerly Spring Break central, the Elbo Room has actually managed to maintain its rowdy and divey reputation by serving up frequent drink specials and live bands. Ironically, it was almost torn down until the Penrod family of chic and sleek Nikki Beach fame bought the place to keep it alive. No matter what, it'll always be a beloved dive. Open daily from 10am to 2am.

EXIT 66
219 S. Fort Lauderdale Beach Blvd., Fort Lauderdale: 954-357-9981

http://m.exit66fl.com
WEBSITE DOWN AT PRESSTIME
Pool Party: open every weekend from 1pm until dark.
Located 1/2 block North of Las Olas Blvd and A1A.

ORIGINAL FAT CAT'S
320 Himmarshee St., Fort Lauderdale: 954-467-5867
They have a Facebook page
Popular downtown dive bar rocking out to live local
bands every night. Great place for those who need a
break from the booty music found in most other
clubs. Widest Craft Beer selection in all of Broward.
Happy Hour 5pm-10pm and live entertainment daily.
21+ only.

THE PARROT
911 Sunrise Lane, Fort Lauderdale: 954-563-1493
http://www.parrotlounge.com
WEBSITE DOWN AT PRESSTIME
Fort Lauderdale's most famous dive bar, The Parrot is
a local's and out-of-towner's choice for an evening of
beer (16 kinds on tap), bonding, and browsing the
bar's gallery of photos of almost everyone who's ever
imbibed here since its opening in 1970. Open Sunday
through Thursday from 11am to 2am, and Friday and
Saturday from 11am to 3am.

THE POOR HOUSE
110 SW 3rd Ave., Fort Lauderdale: 954-522-5145
http://www.poorhousebar.com
There's nothing poor about this microbrew hangout,
where excellent live music by local bands starts at
midnight and goes on well into the wee hours. A
friendly, lively, mixed crowd composes a
generational cross section where the gap is bridged by
a common love of music, cold beer, and good times.
Open nightly from 6pm-4am.

POSH LOUNGE
110 N. Federal Hwy, Fort Lauderdale: 954-763-3553
http://www.poshlasolas.com
Posh Lounge incorporates contemporary decor with
an extensive wine list, Mediterranean tapas, hookahs
and a resident DJ to create a unique and stylish
atmosphere.

REVOLUTION LIVE
100 SW 3rd Ave., Fort Lauderdale: 954-449-1025
www.jointherevolution.net

Some of today's hottest indie bands play here, but if you're not into live music, fret not because this cavernous place is a dance club, too. Open Thursday to Sunday until 4am. Opening hours and cover charges vary, depending on what band is playing.

RHYTHM & VINE
401 NE 5th Terrace, Fort Lauderdale, 954-533-3734
www.rhythm-vine.com
Dance Club featuring a little beer garden with rotating food trucks. Live DJ. Food menu features comfort food bites like BBQ & Mac and cheese. Closed Mon & Tues.

ROCK BAR
219 S Fort Lauderdale Beach Blvd., Fort Lauderdale: 954-728-9804
www.itsbetteronthebeach.com/rock-bar
When you want to pick up the energy and turn up the volume step up to Rock Bar. This rockin' beach bar offers a typical American menu and an oceanfront setting. 2-for-1 margaritas and drink specials daily. If you don't feel like leaving after your meal, Rock Bar also offers a hookah menu and live entertainment on the weekends.

ROUND UP COUNTRY WESTERN BAR
9020 W State Rd. 84, Davie: 954-423-1990
http://www.roundupnightclub.com
Known world wide for its country western dancing (Two Step, Line Dance, Cha Cha, East Coast Swing, West Coast Swing), and live entertainment. Full service restaurant with a full dinner menu.

SEMINOLE HARD ROCK HOTEL & CASINO
1 Seminole Way, Hollywood: 866-502-7529
http://www.seminolehardrockhollywood.com
When it comes to nightlife in these parts, some of the
hottest lounges and clubs are located within this
mega-complex. Among them, Pangaea and Gryphon,
opened by a NYC nightlife impresario, and Opium,
which -- gasp -- crossed the county line from Miami
and was followed by its faithful disciples of A-listers
and club kids spanning the tricounty area. Also here:
popular dance club Passion, Murphy's Law Irish Pub,
Automatic Slim's, and more.

SHO NIGHTCLUB
15 W Las Olas Blvd., Fort Lauderdale: 954-462-3322
Mixing a state-of-the-art sound system and over-the-
top décor bringing partygoers into a sleek and stylish
atmosphere. The legendary nightlife location brings a
high-energy decadent atmosphere complete with
outstanding sound. Music appeals to all patrons, with
a mix of house, hip-hop and open format. Open four
nights a week, Thurs–Sat, 9pm to 4am. Thursday
nights, guests can enjoy open format for the Electric
Karma Party. Fridays will include House and
Saturday's guests can enjoy the best open format sets
in town. SHO will also be opening the second level of
its club for Industry Tuesdays.

SHOOTERS
3033 NE 32nd Ave, Fort Lauderdale: 954-566-2855
www.shooterswaterfront.com

This waterfront bar is quintessential Fort Lauderdale. Inside you'll find nautical types, families, and young professionals mixed with a good dose of sunburned tourists enjoying the live reggae, jazz, or Jimmy Buffett-style tunes, with the gorgeous backdrop of the bay and marinas all around. Open Monday through Friday from 11:30am to 2am, Saturday from 11:30am to 3am, and Sunday from 10am to 2am.

WRECK BAR
B Ocean
1140 Seabreeze Blvd., Fort Lauderdale: 954-524-5551
www.bhotelsandresorts.com
Reconnect in the unique Wreck Bar, an iconic favorite for decades serving cocktails and light fare. Open daily from 5:30pm-12:00am. Live mermaid show at the iconic Wreck Bar every Friday at 6pm, bring the kids, this kind of show is perfect for someone young.

YOLO
333 E. Las Olas Blvd., Fort Lauderdale: 954-523-1000
www.yolorestaurant.com
From happy hour habitués to night owls, O-lounge provides a unique vibe in a polished setting that glows as the night progresses. It's a comfortable gathering spot that feels trendy but without being pretentious. Here you can people watch, talk with friends and enjoy DJs mixing and blending funk, lounge and retro music.

Chapter 5
ATTRACTIONS

AQUATIC ADVENTURES BOAT RENTAL
301 Seabreeze Blvd., Ft Lauderdale, 954-459-8020
www.aquaticboatrental.com
FEES: Costs based on what you do. They offer kite surfing, kayaking, parasailing or you can rent one of their powerboats. They operate trips and tours by the hour, half day and full day with all the water sports equipment included. The service also provides free

transportation to and from area hotels. There's a kite surfing school here.

BILLIE SWAMP SAFARI
30000 Gator Tail Trl., Clewiston, 863-983-6101
www.billieswamp.com/
ADMISSION: fee varies
This is an up-close-and-personal look into the Seminole reservation. Daily tours into the wetlands and hardwood hammocks where you can see deer, water buffalo, bison, wild hogs, ornery ostriches, rare birds, and alligators in their natural habitat. You can also stay overnight in a native Tiki hut for a fee.

BONNET HOUSE
900 N. Birch Rd., Fort Lauderdale: 954-563-5393
http://www.bonnethouse.org
ADMISSION: fee varies
Historic 35-acre plantation home and estate. You can only go through it with a guided tour, however, you

might want to ask about the love story associated with this place. Beautiful grounds, whimsical artwork and interesting design.

BUTTERFLY WORLD
3600 W. Sample Rd., Ft. Lauderdale: 954-977-4400
http://www.butterflyworld.com
ADMISSION: $25 adults and seniors, $20 children ages 3-11.
Everything Butterfly. Kids especially love the Bug Museum which allows them to interact with little critters, with the assistance of well trained employees.

FORT LAUDERDALE ANTIQUE CAR MUSEUM
1527 S.W. 1st Ave., Fort Lauderdale: 954-779-7300
www.antiquecarmuseum.net
ADMISSION: fee varies
Boy, will you be surprised at what you'll see inside. They have a very nice collection of automobiles,

including many Packards, from limousines to speedsters. Photography is allowed.

FORT LAUDERDALE SUN TROLLEY
290 NE 3rd Av, Fort Lauderdale: 954-761-3543
http://www.suntrolley.com
Small fee
This is a great way to get around downtown Fort Lauderdale and the beaches. It's convenient and inexpensive. They also offer an all-day pass. Can't beat that.

GULFSTREAM PARK RACING & CASINO
901 South Federal Hwy, Hallandale Beach: 954-454-7000
http://www.gulfstreampark.com
Admission: Free to the park.
South Florida's premier thoroughbred racetrack, home of the foremost Triple Crown prep races including the Florida Derby. The nation's finest 3-year old thoroughbreds, jockeys and trainers spend their winter at Gulfstream Park. Slots, poker and other casino action spread out over two casino floors, adjacent to the historic Gulfstream Park racetrack. Open 365 days a year; 850 slot machines, electronic table games and hi-stakes poker.

HILLSBORO INLET LIGHTHOUSE
907 Hillsboro Mile, Hillsboro Beach, 954-942-2102
http://www.hillsborolighthouse.org
ADMISSION: fee varies
Standing 136 feet above water, this lighthouse marks the

northern end of the Florida Reef. It contains a 5,500,000-candlepower light and is the most powerful light on the East Coast of the United States. There's an interesting story attached to this landmark, the disappearance of barefoot mailman James Hamilton, which to this day remains a mystery.

HUGH TAYLOR BIRCH STATE PARK
3109 E. Sunrise Blvd., Fort Lauderdale: 954-564-4521
www.floridastateparks.org/park/Hugh-Taylor-Birch
ADMISSION: fee varies
Picnicking, camping, bike rental, swimming and canoeing smack dab in the middle of the city. This 180-acre park offers a calming getaway from the hustle and bustle of the city. The value of this

resource to Fort Lauderdale can't be overestimated. I used to drive by it year after year until I took my first step inside. The fact that it was preserved and not developed is the biggest surprise. But here you'll get a feeling what the area looked like to early settlers.

INTERNATIONAL SWIMMING HALL OF FAME
1 Hall of Fame Dr., Fort Lauderdale: 954-462-6536
http://www.ishof.org
ADMISSION: fee varies
The museum houses the world's largest collection of water-related memorabilia and in the store, you will find anything and everything related to the aquatic sport. One of the best spots in Fort Lauderdale to get the kind of souvenirs you really won't find anywhere else.

Ft. Lauderdale's Legendary Riverboat

Fun-Filled Sightseeing - "The Venice of America"

JUNGLE QUEEN RIVERBOAT
Bahia Mar Boating Center, 801 Seabreeze Blvd., Fort Lauderdale: 954-462-5596

http://www.junglequeen.com
ADMISSION: check web site
Cruise along the waterways of Fort Lauderdale as you
enjoy a BBQ dinner and show onboard this old world
riverboat. This old boat has been plying the
waterways here for decades, and it's the ultimate
touristy thing to do in Fort Lauderdale, but just get
over it and go do it. It's not nearly as touristy as the
Duck Tour! And here, you get a decent meal while
you tour the waterways. To come to Fort Lauderdale
and not see the waterways is to miss one of the great
things about the town. It's just a matter of how you
want to experience it: hire a private boat, go on the
Duck Tour, do the Jungle Queen.

LADY HELEN FISHING CHARTERS
1534 SE 15th St. #3, Fort Lauderdale: 954-336-3256
http://www.ladyhelencharters.com
FEES: check web site
Private fishing charters for up to 4 anglers on the 29'
twin diesel sport fisherman the "Lady Helen."
Children are welcome and encouraged to participate.
Full safety equipment. Many years ago, South Florida
used to be a fisherman's heaven. But the business is
no longer as vital as it used to be. With the dearth of
charter fishing boats, one wonders about the
"sustainable fish" you read about on pompous menus
in fancy restaurants. Whenever I go on one of these
trips, I always release the fish after it's caught.

LAS OLAS BOULEVARD
Fort Lauderdale

Very popular and quaint street located in downtown Fort Lauderdale. Here you will find good food and good shopping, along a few historical points of interest. Shopping includes boutiques, art galleries and antique stores.

LAS OLAS RIVERFRONT
Andrews Ave. at SE 2nd St., Fort Lauderdale
This was once a very nice place to spend an afternoon and evening. It is now a mere shadow of its former self and maybe not even that good. You can pick up the water taxi there which is nice and there is a very good river cruise boat, but that's about it. In the evening, it is a hangout for rude kids and panhandlers.

MAI-KAI POLYNESIAN DINNER SHOW
3599 N Federal Hwy, Fort Lauderdale: 954-563-3272
http://www.maikai.com
ADMISSION: there's a fee for the show
The roaring drums mark the beginning of the exciting "island revue." It's about as phony now as it was a hundred years ago when they first came up with this concept of a "romantic Hawaiian wedding dance" and the "thrilling Samoan fire knife dance performed by our native Polynesian dancers." To read it, you want to barf. But trust me, it's a lot of fun. And the food's good, too.

Ready for Adventure?
Our incredible food and shows take you there!

MCGINNIS WATERSKI
2421 SW 46 Ave., Fort Lauderdale: 954-214-2792
www.mcski.com
FEES: Beginner lesson: fee varies
This place is really great and teaches those who want
to learn as well as help to improve the skills of those
who already know how to ski. Call to reserve.

MUSEUM OF DISCOVERY & SCIENCE
401 SW 2nd St., Fort Lauderdale: 954-467-6637
http://www.mods.org
ADMISSION: fee varies
Although the museum is geared towards children,
adults won't feel like they're in a kiddie museum. The
IMAX theatre is really something to experience.

NSU ART MUSEUM
1 E. Las Olas Blvd., Fort Lauderdale: 954-525-5500
www.nsuartmuseum.org
ADMISSION: fee varies

With more than 200 paintings; 50 sculptures and1,200 works on paper, this is truly a fantastic modern-art facility. They also showcase more than 90 Cuban artists in exile around the world. With traveling exhibits and continuing art classes, the museum offers free admission from 5 to 8pm on the third Thursday of every month.

OLD FORT LAUDERDALE VILLAGE & MUSEUM
219 SW Second Ave., Fort Lauderdale: 954-463-4431
http://www.fortlauderdalehistorycenter.org
WEBSITE DOWN AT PRESSTIME
ADMISSION: fee varies
This is a terrific place to go whether you're a tourist or a local. This place is rich with the fun history of Fort Lauderdale. Great for history buffs.

STRANAHAN HOUSE
335 SE 6th Ave., Fort Lauderdale: 954-524-4736
http://www.stranahanhouse.org
ADMISSION fee varies

A worthwhile little museum of South Florida pioneer life, this is Fort Lauderdale's oldest standing structure. It is filled with turn-of-the-20th-century furnishings and historical photos of the area.

WATER TAXI
All over Fort Lauderdale: 954-467-6677
https://watertaxi.com/
ADMISSION: fee varies
Unlimited rides all day in Fort Lauderdale and Hollywood.
This is a particularly nice way to get around the main hub of Fort Lauderdale. You get a very different perspective of this town from its waterways that snake through its beautiful neighborhoods with a great view of the city's most beautiful homes. Check the website for schedules and stops.

XTREME ACTION PARK
5300 N. Powerline Rd., Fort Lauderdale: 954-491-6265
www.xtremeactionpark.com
ADMISSION: varies
Just as the name says, this is the fastest indoor go karting around. This is an excellent facility with a friendly staff. Lots of fun.

YOUNG AT ART CHILDREN'S MUSEUM
751 SW 125th Ave., Davie: 954-424-0085
www.youngatartmuseum.org/
Admission fee varies
Any day you drop into the museum will be fun as they have different classes, workshops and exhibit.

Very educational with areas like Earthworks that teaches children about recycling and repurposing and Global Village that teaches about different cultures through art, music and play.

Chapter 6
SHOPPING & SERVICES

BARNES & NOBLE BOOKSTORE
2051 N. Federal Hwy., Fort Lauderdale: 954-561-3732
http://www.barnesandnoble.com
Two-story mega bookstore has a Starbucks Coffee with tasty desserts.

BASS PRO SHOPS OUTDOOR WORLD
200 Gulf Stream Way, Dania Beach: 954-929-7710
http://www.basspro.com
This store has an indoor water feature that showcases
fish species that are indigenous to the area. The fish
in their tanks are game fish of great size. In some of
these aquariums, professional anglers and store staff
hold demonstrations showing the use of artificial bait.
They catch the fish in these tanks to show how well
the bait works. Bass Pro Shops is also known for its
Outdoor Skills Workshops, teaching skills as varied
as fly fishing, Dutch oven cooking, archery hunting
with an archery range in the store, and GPS
navigation. They hold many "skill workshops" with
the top names in the outdoor world. One of the really
unique places to visit in the Fort Lauderdale not
duplicated elsewhere in the country.

WESTFIELD BROWARD MALL
8000 W. Broward Blvd., Plantation: 954-473-8100
www.westfield.com/broward
Very nice mall, with Macy's, Dillards, Sears. Even
Sears Auto. Nail and hair salon. Food court has the
usual "variety," but nothing you've not seen before.
Cuban to pizza to Chinese. Has lots of sales.

CORAL RIDGE MALL
3200 N. Federal Hwy., Fort Lauderdale: 954-537-
2700
http://www.mycoralridgemall.com
You'll find values galore along with a wide range of
services, food and entertainment at the Coral Ridge

Mall. Centrally located in Greater Fort Lauderdale with easy access to the beaches. The mall is home to more than 40 stores and terrific prices and selections. Shop Target, Marshalls, HomeGoods, Old Navy, TJ Maxx, GNC, Payless ShoeSource, Bath & Body Works, Game Stop, Nine West, Footlocker, Easy Spirit and Motherhood Maternity just to name a few, plus Einstein Bros. Bagels, Jamba Juice, Galaxy Pizza, Publix and much more. Or stop by at AMC Movie Theatres for a cool escape.

DESIGN CENTER OF THE AMERICAS (DCOTA)
1855 Griffin Rd., Dania Beach: 954-920-7997
http://www.dcota.com
A 775,000-square-foot interior-design center with furniture showrooms (featuring everything from ultramod to classic), designer studios, and, from time to time, fabulous sample sales.

DOLLAR TREE
1391 SE 17th St., Fort Lauderdale: 954-991-7649
http://www.dollartree.com
A true dollar store. Everything's $1. (Well, almost.) Among the many, many items here you will find stuff like name brand toothpaste. But if you're not shopping for toothpaste, you will definitely find something you need. Clean and well-organized store.

FORT LAUDERDALE SWAP SHOP

3291 W. Sunrise Blvd., Fort Lauderdale: 954-791-7927

www.floridaswapshop.com

This is a Flea Market but done on a much grander scale than any other flea market. About the only thing you can't find here are high prices. They have just about everything from fresh produce, trashy junk, a few high-end items, restaurants, car displays, drive-in movies, and sometimes, a circus show. (In fact, this place is a circus.)

GALLERIA MALL

2414 East Sunrise Blvd., Fort Lauderdale: 954-564-1015

http://www.galleriamall-fl.com

This is the place for Lauderdale's high-end shoppers. You make do here until you can visit Bal Harbour in Miami or Palm Beach. In fact, one of the reasons Fort Lauderdale doesn't have a huge number of high-end boutiques and specialty stores is because it lies so conveniently between Miami and Palm Beach, both of which have plenty of the best shopping in the world. The Galleria is anchored by three major department stores: Neiman Marcus, Macy's and Dillard's. Other famous retailers and specialty shops include Apple, Coach, Mayor's, Willams-Sonoma, Cole Haan, J.Crew and Pottery Barn. The Galleria is also a premier Fort Lauderdale dining destination, with restaurants like **Capital Grille, P.F. Chang's, Seasons 52, Blue Martini and Trulucks.**

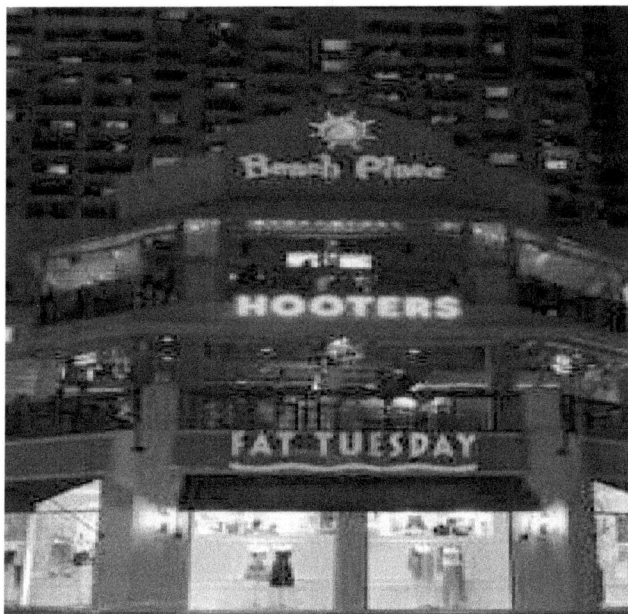

GALLERY AT BEACH PLACE

17 S. Fort Lauderdale Beach, Fort Lauderdale: 954-760-9570

http://www.galleryatbeachplace.com

The area's only beachfront mall is located in Fort Lauderdale on Florida A1A just north of Las Olas Boulevard. This 100,000-square-foot giant has the usual chains, such as Sunglass Hut, as well as chain bars and restaurants such as Hooter's. While views of the ocean are fantastic, the shopping isn't so great, with only about 12 stores, one of them being a CVS Pharmacy that is open 24 hrs.

IKEA

151 NW 136th Ave., Sunrise: 888-888-4532

http://www.ikea.com/us/en/store/sunrise

The 20-acre Ikea store features exclusively designed items, three model homes, 50 room settings, a supervised children's play area, as well as a restaurant serving Swedish specialties as well as American dishes.

JEZEBEL
1980 E. Sunrise Blvd., Fort Lauderdale: 954-761-7881
They have a Facebook page
This funky, adorable shop is chock full of hip gifts, oodles of cards, designer and vintage clothing and accessories, and so much more. At Jezebel you'll find everything from stylish candles and home decor to funky jewelry and t-shirts, and everything in between.

LAS OLAS BOULEVARD
A block east of Federal Hwy. (US 1, off SE 8th St.), Fort Lauderdale
http://www.lasolasboulevard.com
Las Olas isn't just a street. The Boulevard begins with the Museum of Art at No. 1, and goes right down to the **Elbo Room** on A1A. In between the two are the businesses and organizations that you'd find in any other community in America; restaurants of all types, salons, banks, realtors, gas stations, a barbershop, a post office, a pharmacy, a deli, sidewalk cafes, jewelry stores, a cigar bar, antiques stores, art stores, fashion boutiques, a bakery, churches, shoe stores, a diner, a hotel, liquor stores, and even their own historic house.

LAS OLAS OUTDOOR GOURMET MARKET

1201 SE Las Olas Blvd., Fort Lauderdale
www.themarketcompany.org
This is a year-round open-air market featuring
gourmet-style fruits and vegetables, organics,
culinary herbs, tropical plants and orchids, fresh
baked breads and pastries, local honey, handmade
soaps, gourmet pastas, sauces and dressings, stone
crabs in season, dog treats, and God knows what else.

LAS OLAS RIVERFRONT

Andrews Ave. at SE 2nd St., Fort Lauderdale: 954-
522-6556
This was once a very nice place to spend an afternoon
and evening. It is now a mere shadow of its former
self and maybe not even that good. Only one decent
restaurant still exists, the **Briney Pub.** You can pick
up the water taxi there which is nice and there is a
very good river cruise boat, but that's about it. In the
evening, it is a hangout for rude kids and panhandlers.

OUT OF THE CLOSET
1785 E. Sunrise Blvd., Fort Lauderdale: 954-462-9442
www.outofthecloset.org
This place has really nice, gently used stuff. Clothes, furniture and knick-knacks for great prices. Every day there is a different sale, depending on the tag color. Sometimes you can get stuff for $1. All their proceeds go to AIDS/HIV research and you can also get a free HIV test after you shop.

RADIO-ACTIVE RECORDS
845 N. Federal Hwy., Fort Lauderdale: 954-762-9488
http://radio-active-records.tumblr.com
It's a bit bigger than your average record store. Pretty evenly split between new and used stuff. Carrying both CDs and Vinyl, with a pretty nice selection of niche stuff; such as local bands, garage, and psychedelic. Two turntables in the corner allow you to sample everything you're interested in buying.

SAWGRASS MILLS MALL
12801 W. Sunrise Blvd., Sunrise: 954-846-2300
http://www.simon.com/mall/?id=1262
Passionate shoppers can be assured they'll find absolutely everything here: from electronics, fashion, shoes, surf wear and boards (one of the largest **Ron Jon's Surf Shops** is located here) to art prints, there's virtually nothing you couldn't find at Sawgrass Mills. Besides shopping, there are plenty of entertainment options such as a multiplex movie theater with 23

cinemas and countless restaurants ranging from Burger King to **Wolfgang Puck**.

YELLOW GREEN FARMERS MARKET
1940 North 30th Rd., Hollywood: 954-513-3990
www.ygfarmersmarket.com
All under one outdoor roof, Yellow Green is a true farmer's market providing a bounty of seasonal, fresh foods along with artisanal goods created by local artists and craftsmen. Come support and chat with local farmers and gain a deeper understanding of the many healthful and environmental benefits of seasonal eating.

INDEX

* 9 7 8 1 3 9 3 1 4 1 8 9 1 *